POEMS FROM
THE HEART

POEMS FROM
THE HEART

Jonetta W. Singleton

To order additional copies of this book, contact:
Xlibris Corporation
1-888-795-4274
www.Xlibris.com
Orders@Xlibris.com
20625

CONTENTS

PREFACE

Two constant companions inspired me to publish this book, *Poems from the Heart*. Some were written before the age of six. Pencil and paper were my two friends.

They were my play toys.

No matter how hard I tried to engage in other activities, the pencil and paper would always be near me.

I consider myself a world traveler and a bookworm.

These poems stem from the observations, feelings and love in my life from early childhood to senior citizenship

I fervently hope this book will inspire older people everywhere to realize their creative talent.

I was encouraged to publish these poems by Mr. Johnny Smith, who was a Baltimore City school principal for over 40 years. Christopher Powers, Ph.D., assisted in the preparation of the book.

I would like to dedicate this book to my late husband, Lafayette Singleton, Sr.; my son, Dr. Lafayette Singleton, Jr.; my daughter Carrie E. Singleton, a counselor in the Baltimore City Public School system; my two grandchildren, Laura M. Singleton, attorney, and Lorin Singleton, a professional photographer; Mercedes Hughes, my niece; Kathryn McDugall, my cousin; and Robert Campbell, my nephew.

Jonetta W. Singleton

A DREAM

Oh, for a thought so extreme
Who could love the world so dearly
And captivate its worth so clearly?
Only God gives sense to a dream

Only God can give us a gleam
Of the worthiness of the heart
To a worried soul God does his part
In all creation, this is God's theme

A dream is a wish and a goal
A dream is Heaven-sent
A message given in bold
To straighten a soul that is bent
Turn it to the path that is right
To receive God's purest delight

LONELY HEART

Out of the lonely heart
The mind makes contact with the intimate:
The God that always does his part,
And holds the reins in any fate.

Out of a lonely heart
God gives the answers private and real;
He wanted silence from the start,
For you to meditate and feel.

Out of a lonely heart
Inspiration invigorates the soul;
Gives birth to the enduring art
While genius oppresses its soul.

Out of a lonely heart
Love is so enchantingly manifested;
It is real with not a flirt,
With honesty and loyalty all invested.

A ROSE

One day I clipped a rose
and placed it in a vase;
Its beauty you couldn't oppose,
A winner it would be in any race.

A day or two went by;
The petals began to fall
As its life started a peaceful end,
Answering the Master's call.

The death of the rose leaves an imprint:
Its lesson will never be erased.
The charm of its truth:
Today we live, yet tomorrow we are erased!

But its beauty is a lingering memory,
Its love is everlasting;
Its life is gone and just a memory
Its seeds of hope will go everlasting!

A SONG TO SELF

The echoes from my voice sound like a bell
Unmodulated and with a keen comprehension
Of the great it will foretell
That God's freedom is without apprehension

As my heart tries to be numb and still
But sometimes overtaken by piles of stress
Waiting patiently for dreams to fill
With God's blessings and nothing less

Some days are cumbersome and long
And injustice seems senseless and wrong
For justice seems bleak and out of reach
No words of kindness and fairness to preach

When men cry out for liberty
When the whole world rejoices in the trinity
God the Father, the Son, and the Holy Spirit
We will all be saved, that is our merit.

A STAR

I saw a star, a beautiful star
Dancing across the sky
I saw this so radiant and far
It seamed so near, but yet high
It was just dancing across the sky

I wondered why, but I seemed to think
The star someday, I could reach
And pondered the thought link by link
Digging my hands in sand on the beach

I thought very hard, why I fell in love
With such an unreachable star
So radiantly sparkling like a diamond above
To myself, it is only a dream, it is not far.

1 know that someday and not very long
I will reach this unreachable star
For my faith is steadfast and my mind is strong
To get my wish, I would break any bar.

A Thing of Beauty

I saw a beautiful bird
Flying freely in the sky
Before I could speak a word
He had dashed away so high

His beauty has left an imprint
It is for all the world to see
The gift that nature has lent
And not to be coveted just by me

The beauty of the bird I cannot claim
Nor can I catch him and put him in a cage
He is of eternal fame
To be loved and praised by any age

The bird like all things of beauty
Whether in nature or in the soul
Gives the responsibility and duty
To appreciate nature's wonders as they unfold.

A THOUGHT

When the wind strikes like ice
Blowing from some distant Alaskan sky
And your nose and hand are frostbitten
The tears from your eyes freeze as you cry

When the sun shines and burns the trees
The grass and the beautiful flowers
They are warm as bathing pools
Your hopes seem to be in vain, as you wish for
an April shower

When a single year seems like two
A month, a day, seems never to end
The agony of ice and the pains of stone seem to haunt you
And you dream of happiness to close in around the bend

You clasp your hand and wait for the peace
The wheel of fortune to bring happiness in,
For your heart of love is prepared
To be a giver and not just the receiver to the end.

A TREE

Why do you stand so erect?
Why do you give so much beauty
Is it your service to protect
And nestle the birds; is that your duty?

Why do you stand year in and year out,
Sheltering strangers from sun and rain?
Why do you spread your branches about
To make an umbrella for human gain?

Why do you give so much
And receive so little?
While men do not value you as such
And harm you, and not a little?

You are something that God made;
He fed your roots with heavenly waters;
Your trunk grows, you give shade,
Your willingness to serve is all that matters.

A VISIT TO GRANDMA'S HOUSE

A visit to Grandma's house was a treat
For all the adventures we would meet
The crayfish gumbo and homemade cakes
Spread with icing and marmalade

The washing of the clothes was a chore
Boiled in a black iron pot I had never seen before
Rinsed in the bayou and hung on the fence
Made of barbed wire for the cattle's defense

The riding of horses and the chasing of cattle
The running in the woods and the shining of the saddle
The killing of hogs, and the smoking of meat
Not so much to do in winter, but plenty to eat

On Sundays, there was Sunday school
So each child could learn the golden rules
Back from church to eat fried chicken
That Granny carefully prepared in the kitchen

Granny could give a look with her eyes
Enough to send me sailing to the skies
She used no strap or switch
Just one look from her eyes would do the trick

Granny is sleeping well today
Again, she will never pass this way
But as I look back in my mind
Granny was the greatest angel one could find.

A Withered Rose Bush

My little rosebush will bloom
It isn't completely dead
There is no need for gloom
God his own has always fed

God will sprinkle each leaf
With little bits of sun and rain
He will give each little leaf
What nature intended to cure its pain

I shall watch constantly for a bud
A white one, red, yellow, and pink
Just a simple little rosebush
To pluck and to hold as I think

With each flower that I pluck from it
I will never forget the God that made it grow
Each moment of beauty that I get from it
I shall be thankful to God for making it grow.

AFRICA

Out from Africa here we are;
Chained into slavery, there was no law;
No mercy shown-worked, beaten and scolded
A life of devastation and hardships unfolded.

No stable family unit to protect us;
No language worth saving but the select;
A new god, and an earthly master;
A whip, a plow—with that we were worked faster.

Bore children not really to keep;
But to be put on the block and sold like sheep;
No wife or husband to form a union of one;
No permanent home to dwell when the day was done.

The spiritual songs—words were easy to find;
And at night the reels would come to mind;
The dances at sundown;
And the ears that always listened for the master's sound.

The master's children's lesson in the classroom;
The still, quiet sweep of the broom;
The spelling of words to keep in the head;
And a closed memory of every word read.

The hiding of books and notes on paper;
The concealing of learning was a terrible caper;
To act dumb and yet not be dumb;
Always keep the right action at the thumb.

To learn to read and create a word of thought;
The thoughts that multiply more than has been taught;
The questions, oh the questions of freedom and equality;
The questions, the questions of justice and liberty.

Alarming desire deep down in the heart;
To share your learning as your part;
To create solid friendships and family ties;
And to begin now or time flies.

A burning desire to express ideas;
A burning desire to express how one feels;
And how to steadfastly push for the freedom objective;
Always being honest, forthright and un-subjective.

AN EVERGREEN TREE

Of all the trees in the forest
I would like to be an evergreen
To me she is stable and erect
So dignified, and always seen.

She greets the summer and winter the same;
She greets the March wind with her bursting frame
And welcomes the spring, so fair, the same
She welcomes the snow to embed in her mane.

She greets the summer in her array of green
Untarnished by the season
Her branches sparkle with gleam
And her power to grow — only God knows the reason.

The evergreen will forever be green,
Only God can make it so
She's a lesson power unseen
Who keeps her green, who makes her grow?

BEAUTY

Outward beauty is pleasant to see
But it is not permanent, it's somewhat magical
The forces of nature will cause it to flee
As it fades with age, it becomes farcical

Outward beauty is not enough
A rose is to smell
Not to lust forever: bid it farewell

Inward beauty is in the heart
There are no fragments to decay
It cannot be seen, but it is there
And not a piece of art

Inward beauty is eternal
It is a God-given gift
Love, goodness and kindness are eternal
And glow outside without a rift.

BEFORE I ASK HIS FORGIVENESS

If I have injured or broken someone's heart
If I have left the lonely by the roadside
If I have not practiced love's healing art
May the sun not go down before I ask forgiveness.

If I have failed to help some lone sparrow
Take a flight to the sky again
If I cannot hang my head in sorrow
For someone's unbearable pain,
May the sun not go down before I ask forgiveness.

If I fail to soothe someone burdened with a heavy load
Or dry the tears from weeping eyes
If I fail to put a wanderer on the right road
Or fail to soothe the orphan's cries
May the sun not go down before I ask forgiveness.

If I have spoken an unkind word
If I have walked in the wrong path
If I have not fed even a little bird, and
Failed to tell what God hath
May the sun not go down before I ask forgiveness.

Birth

The young was entwined in fears
She used her hair to wipe her tears
Her head was drooped with hands so cold
There was not a whisper in her soul
Her face showed grief, and called for heavenly relief
For the pain was slow and time was slow
And she wondered and prayed who could suffer more

But sure to come, for every soul to welcome
A newborn child, not sprung from the wild
But from a place blessed in itself
Who was taught a great lesson.
Out of pain, good is born.

BLACK MAN

Black man
Your neck is suspended from a tree
Your ma and pa are crying
Your wife, your kid, nowhere to turn.

Black man
Your preacher says your soul is in heaven
Your wife and children are hungry
Your preacher says God will provide.

Black man
Your children will grow up with scars.
Your wife is the great matriarch
Your sons will follow your fate
Your daughter, another matriarch.

Black man
Your ghost returns from the grave
Your ghost daring the klan-hood
Your sons are demanding your rights
Your daughter is at home with her brood.

Black man
Your wife is leading many fights
Your wife is fighting for equal rights
Your cherished dreams are realized
That you are at last a man among men
You have gained equality at last.

CHRISTMAS

When the last pie is in the oven
And the last cake is ready to bake
The turkey has been dressed and topped with cover
And only the plum pudding to make

When the stockings have been hung in the fireplace
And the tree is glowing with balls and lights
Mom is tired but has an angel's face
Because she has done the best with all her might.

The candles are in the windows, oh how they glow
Sending their radiance all over the place,
The holly wreaths on the door
And decorations all over the place.

And, alas, everywhere it is still
The whistling is still without a sound
The whole scene is filled with good will,
Peace and rejoicing all around.

The distant voices carols are singing
Window shades are raised
The door is cracked to see the mingling
To give honor to the wonder we have praised.

Covet

The one that I love so dear
Made my heart throb a little bit;
The one that I wanted to be near
And into his heart make a hit.

The one that had taken my soul
Garnered up my heart and taken it away;
The one that had owned all of me so bold
Held me so tight I couldn't sway.

But who was the one that I cherished so dear?
In my dreams he always haunted me;
God does not make life such
That another can destroy another's soul, you see!

You see, we should not covet at all
A lover that belongs to another;
If we do, it is surely our downfall —
It is unfair to want what belongs to another.

Dancing

Oh take this chance
So my limber feet can dance
As the music plays my favorite waltz
Oh my honey, you're the boss

Oh take this chance
And do a little prance
As we do a dance beneath the moon
One night of happiness and not of doom

One gaze at the star
One kiss

DANCING WITH SADIE

In my sleep I dream
That I am dancing with Sadie
The girl I hold so close in my dream
I dance the two-step with my lady.

I dance as her face touches mine
I touch her lips, feel her embrace
The sleep I remember is so divine
As I stare into her diamond eyes and face.

I pray that I should never be awakened
As long as I am with my fair lady
All the world I have forsaken
Just to remain in my dream with Sadie.

Day will come, but I'll push it away
I can't afford to lose my Sadie
A Lombardi tune, a thought of May
When love is in bloom for me and my lady.

Day's End

Shower me with roses
Before this lovely day closes
Put them in every room
Before the nighttime gloom

Keep water fresh and pure
Keep the farewell short but sure
When life reaches its last ebbing tide
And enters everlasting life to abide

For I have done my best in every way
Kindness, love, and hope filled my day
So as I close my eyes and say goodbye
Don't let a tear fall from your eye
For I have lived my life in God's beauty
I was happy in going about God's duty.

DEAR GOD

Teach me to love my fellow man
As we meet from day to day;
Give me the gift to be a kindly human
As I travel through life's narrow way

Give me that push to go forward,
A light that I may see;
Send me with goodness onward;
Thy mercy, I need all of thee.

Balance my feet, that I may stand,
Open my mouth, that I may speak
Use my soul at thy demand,
Give me ambition for goodness to seek.

Give me a sweet voice
And plenty of songs to sing,
The Scriptures to read of thy choice
And to all, love and kindness bring.

DEAR GOD HOLOCAUST

May there never be another holocaust, nevermore;
No reminder of man's inhumanity to man;
No, there need not be another Hiroshima
To destroy mankind and leave the land barren, nevermore.

Dear God,
May there always be prayers to say
That ask God for freedom, justice, and equality;
And may the world be free of the maladies
As prayer is offered to you in reality.

Dear God,
May all nuclear power and nuclear weapons
Be removed from the face of the earth;
And may man's heart be filled with peace and love,
And may all the children of the world be endowed with
love at birth.

Dear God,
May there be no differences among people—
The last, the first, the rich and the poor;
May all tables be filled with food and love,
And may Your strong hand dominate forevermore.

Don't Kick A Dying Dog

You wouldn't kick a dog that is dying,
Oh, no, not you, I mean you
You who turn away while it is crying
Without giving it a pat or two.

You wouldn't say in a time of need,
"There are more dogs born every day."
You wouldn't say, it has done its last deed
And has to get going down death's way.

You wouldn't say that the dying dog has been no good,
And has only taken up the earth's space;
You wouldn't regard it as rotten wood,
Soon to turn up on the earth's face.

You wouldn't treat a dying dog this way at all:
Today the dog that is left alone to die in pain,
Tomorrow may be well to brace itself without a fall
With a life-filled sun instead of rain.

The dog that was taken to be all washed up yesterday
May find a haven in the world tomorrow;
The dog that suffered with no place to lay,
May find an ending to all its sorrow.

So I say to you, my friends,
Comfort a dog that is dying;
Just as surely as God makes a life that never ends,
Each soul should be good and kind without defying.

Dreams

Now as I lay me down to sleep,
I pray that my guiding angel will keep
A watchful eye over me
And give me dreams as deep as the sea.

May my dreams have God's convictions;
May my dreams have God's reflections
On how His love gives visions
On the highway of forceful missions.

Oh when my eyes are closed in deep sleep,
From memory my dreams I cannot sweep
To be awakened to see the sun or rain
And glance at the horizon over the plain.

With God's love I welcome the dawn;
Days come and go without a frown;
Dreams are real, not only in sleep;
They are God's mind calling from the deep.

FAITH

A good deed comes from the heart
There is no need to share a part
For good comes from within, from the start
God's love and kindness are the art

God sees what happens to wealth
It is better to share it freely than to have it taken
It is better to be thankful for good health
Than to have your faith in silver and gold shaken

Do good regardless of what others say
Tread a straight path every day
Help a lost child find his way
And try to keep a fellowman from going astray.

If the day seems dark and dreary
And the night causes one to feel leery
Joy will come, tomorrow may be merry
A prayer will strengthen the mind so weary.

FATE

Fate, you can't spit on me,
Hit me or push me down the hill
You can't make others forsake me, you see —
No, you can't make me swallow life's bitterest pill

You can't take my sense of love,
My hope, my loyalty and kindness;
My greatest comfort comes from God above,
His blessing and the rest of his fondness

You are just a thing of the future,
Which some sad hearts leave up to you;
But as for me, I am too mature;
I trust in God; he will see me through

Fate, of you, I am not afraid —
All my faith is in God;
My future you cannot raid,
I have all my faith in God.

FLOWERS

I love to pick the wild flowers
On the edge of the forest
I love the smell of flowers after an April shower
To touch and admire nature's best

I love the flowers, they are free from need
They were nourished all on their own
I love them for there is no greed
They fought for life all on their own

I love the wild flowers and their beauty
They stand adorned in all their splendor
They asked for nothing,
But that's their duty

I love the wild flowers in the morning
Their flowers do not last quite long enough
To be exposed to a world of hate
And experience life in the rough

I love wild flowers so fair
Their beauty is a sign that death is near
Death, which we will face someday too.

GAMES WE PLAY

We say that we feel
Like we could run a mile,
But actually we feel as rotten as wood.

Oh, we tell people, "That is lovely,"
And that their attire is in good taste;
We even tell them that their body is lovely,
But we laugh as we turn our heads in haste.

We pretend that we enjoy the music of the highbrow
With friends that we want to impress,
But our thoughts are at the corner bar,
Where we feel comfortable with the unquiet.

We play these games day by day,
Pretending to be what we are not,
We feel funny and guilty along the way,
But this is the way we carry our lot.

GHOST

I call it a phantom or a ghost
He or she, I am its host
It comes when I am sick or sad
Its vibrations make me well and glad

It soothes my pain
It never touches my hand
It guides me like my mother
And tells me to protect my sister and brother

It teaches me to love
It teaches me of the Master above
This gracious company I would miss
All its good vibrations I can list

Dear little ghost, always be near
Your love I can feel in the air
Come to me any day or night
I love to see your sight

God Made Me

My skin is not white like a peach
Not even a pumpkin can compare
But my dark skin is within God's reach
I can feel his touch and sense his welfare

My heart is not filled with greed
That would make me covet what belongs to others
And thus make me fail to concentrate on those in need
Even if it's my brothers or my neighbors

My mind is filled with thoughts of good
Of motivation, of things to learn and do
My heart I never buried in stone or wood
Asking him for the right path for me and you

My mind, my body are at God's call
He tells my tongue when to speak
He guides my feet that I may not fall
His blessed way, I always seek

GONE ARE THE DAYS

When the wind blows
The feathers fly in all yonder way
And then the sun glows
Signaling a halt to the feathers, one by one

Gone are the days when the dragons —
Dressed in remnants white as snow,
Burn crosses to make paragons
For their might to show

Gone are the days when justice sleeps
When might makes right
When voices are crowned and virtues leap
And when the way of the good is out of sight

The day has come for the reward
It is not in heaven, but here
It is not upward or downward
It is here, right here,
In you and me.

Grandma's Possum

Granny skinned a possum, her favorite dish
She washed it and boiled it as done as could be
She gashed it and spiced it to her wish
Then put sweet potatoes around it, a beauty to see

The aroma from that possum began
To spread all over the place, and all around
She put the excess grease in a pan
As we, little children, a new taste had found

Granny was sweet, but she did not share
This possum's meat with the neighborhood
Her grandchildren ah, so fair
The forelegs for that brood

Granny ate the hind legs all up
She ate the potatoes sopped in grease
She washed the pot all up
She now sleeps and dreams with ease.

GREAT MINDS

Great minds cannot be disdained
Nor their thoughts shackled and chained
The ideas are created like a running spring
And put into action by the subject or the king

Spreading the news far and near
That dreams are sound and clean
The task of the mind is at hand
Great minds have invaded the land

They need no artificial props
Their penetration has no stops
The dreams have been accomplished
The task well established
Great minds go through a process
And are able to endure to attain success.

Guess What?

A white man is not what you think he is
And not what he thinks he is;
Saw him in the café eating chitlings
Turnip greens, child, he called chitlings
Some kind of wrinkly steak!

Guess what?
A white man ain't what you think he is
Or what he thinks he is:
Saw him buying an African bush
Trying to say "brother" and "sister"
Just like you

Guess what?
A white man ain't what you think he is
Or what he thinks he is:
He used to call Cadillacs "Nigger Jumpers"
But man, he gives G.M. a lot of business now!

Guess what?
A white man ain't what you think he is
Or what he thinks he is:
He is copying our style of dancing,
He tries his best to sing our jazz
And guess what? He is finally getting to be
A human being!

HOLD TIGHT!

When your crops have almost failed
And there is little or nothing put in store,
When it has thundered and hailed
And you wish time would faster go,
Hold tight! Keep on living.

When your best friend has stabbed you
With a double cross in the back,
Has spit and licked his tongue at you
You suffered and endured the shock,
Hold tight! Keep on living

When success seems to be within reach
Your toils seem to be fulfilling
Then you encounter a leech
Who tries to throw a monkey wrench to do the killing,
Hold tight! Keep on living.

Hope

When moments are filled with desperation
When the mind fails to concentrate on the optimistic
When life is misguided and there is lack of interpretation
You just look to God, He is the greatest mystic

When love seems to hide its face
When you seem left in outer space
When faith seems to be out of place
And all the hurts have fallen on the human race

When church bells give a doleful sound
When the parson lends his voice in prayer
To give praise to God and the heavenly bound
And remind us that God gives answers to prayer

Key words of hope, love and faith are given
They must be abided by day by day
The parson warns that all sins can be forgiven
By using God's only pathway.

HOW DID YOU FEEL
AT GRANDMA'S HOUSE?

I always feel that I am with another child
Exploring a glimpse of life out in the wild
With a playmate so understanding and true
Come and I will share adventures with you

My old grandma stands tall and erect
She watches your manner and corrects
In such a dignified manner you take
Her directions, but rules you never break

She soothes your pain with kisses
She soothes your heartaches, she never misses
She finds your lost toys and your favorite book
She is kind, she has the sweetest look

My granny has a genius mind
She knows everything but she is kind
No secret I would hide from my favorite friend
My grandma will always be with me to the end.

Human

When you are able to elude
A perpetrator or two,
When you are able to conclude
That goodness follows through

When you are able to overlook
Unjust criticism
And find goodness to do
Amid the storm of criticism

When you are able to see the sun
Although the day is dark and dreary,
When you are able to retire when day is done
Peaceful and un-weary

Then you are completely mature,
You are the happy one
You are a plan of nature
The battle you have won.

I AM ME

It is fine that you want me to be the goddess
Of Venus, or even look like you
It is fine that you want me to have the wisdom of Minerva,
And do everything right the day through.

It is fine that you want me to be like Calliope
And sing the lyrics so sweet
It is fine if you want me to be Helen of Troy
But, I am me, just one of the people you meet.

It is fine that you want me to have a Socratic mind
To do inquiries forevermore
It is fine that you want me to travel the world
And see its wonders from shore to shore.

But I have to be the single soul
Created by my parents and the one above
A product of the sun, the total of my environment
Bathed in the beauty of his love
Because . . . I am me.

I DREAMED A NUMBER

Last night in my dream, I saw twenty-one
That morn, I ran to the corner store
I played the number for fifty cents
And wondered if I should play for more.

What do you think? The number came out
By chance, by luck, I don't know
I cried, I smiled, over three hundred dollars
I had never had that luck before.

Now I really started to play the numbers
From one to five dollars a day
One year, two years have passed
I have lost all the way.

Please be smart, and take my advice
The wheel of fortune does not always pay
We can save our time and our funds
And accumulate our fortunes the American way.

I FELL IN LOVE WITH A STAR

I fell in love last night
As I glazed up at the sky
I fell in love with a star so bright
I fell in love, but it's high

I fell in love so fairly
I surely will reach the star
I fell in love so clearly
The star is far, but not so far

If I could hitch my hand
To that dear little shooting star
I would tell every man
That I'm in love with that wonderful star

If I just show my face
To the beautiful star in the sky
He could come to my place
And we could be alone — the star and I.

I Will Weep For A Million Years

If I cannot be truthful with myself
Love myself and have faith in myself
I will weep for a million years.

If I cannot love my friends
At the risk of death, to bitter ends
I will weep for a million years.

If I have bread and my brother has none
If I don't share bread when the day is done
I will weep for a million years.

If I have gold, silver and precious stones
And fail to heed the poor's moans
I will weep for a million years.

If God has given me free will and freedom
And I failed to spread the good news to his kingdom
I will weep for a million years.

ISN'T IT FUNNY

Isn't it funny that blacks kill blacks
Sometimes over a lousy dime crap game
He is much more prone to maim his own
But seldom reach fame

Isn't it funny that some blacks are attracted
To play numbers and take dope
Steal and sell hot goods
These attributes, they can surely cope

Isn't it funny that when a black
Gets his hands on a little money
The biggest car, he surely will buy
Even sleep in it, isn't that funny?

Isn't it funny that some blacks
Are skeptical of other blacks
They will pretend to listen
And to solicit advice from blacks

Isn't it funny that some blacks
Are still Uncle Toms too
Will get all they can snitch
And then laboriously make it hard for you.

Jealousy

Canines don't eat canines
Why should we?
We should rejoice at our brother's good luck
This is the way to feel good, you see.

Why should we try to block someone
Who has worked hard for success?
Why should we try to knock or splatter
Someone's name to excess?

Why should we want it all
And not leave a crumb for anyone?
Why should we rejoice at another's fall
And give him another kick just for fun?

The top of a mountain has a dome
The people you meet going upward
So far away from a familiar home
Are there to meet you when you fall downward.

JUST BECAUSE I AM BLACK

Just because I am black
You use the color of my skin
To deny me of due process
You say that all the human factors I lack

You point to my big feet and kinky hair
You point to my flat nose and big lips
You point to my face and say there's no despair
You say my back is only fit to work and get whips

To compare the difference in you to the difference in me
Is just a fairy tale and at worst a riddle
God's miracle of all human beings, you see
Is the giving of the knowledge that they are a riddle.

Just Endure

My heart is never idle,
It is busy with God's calls,
My soul is never in a riddle,
For truth stands and never falls.

When my pain's too hard to bear,
And fever burns my forehead with sweat,
I still think of the love I shared,
With all the folks I met.

When the terrible heat of the day,
The storms and winters cold,
I only think of a spring or summer day,
When the pleasure enjoyed was so much, untold.

When all the good and bad are weighed,
Justice seems to tip the scale,
The good is there, for I have prayed,
I have no time to sit and wail.

JUST PRAY AND THANK GOD

When you try to give affection
When you try to walk in the right direction
When you give the needed food
And someone misunderstands your mood
Just pray and thank God for it.

When you labor night and day
When your mind is filled with prayer all the way
When lies and jealousy take their turn
From the hard knocks you had to learn
Just pray and thank God for it.

When the world around you seems uncaring
When friends fail to participate in sharing
When love seems to be forgotten
And kind words seem foolish and rotten
Just pray and thank God for it.

When God speaks to the heart
When God makes us aware of our part
When God is able to remind us of others' care
That their burdens we must help with and share
Just pray and thank God for it.

Life Is Like A Rose

Life is a red rose,
Filled with thorns and beauty,
Life, how it grows,
Steadfastly and full of duty.

Life is a rosebud,
Full of youth and vigor,
Soon it will no longer be a bud,
And its beauty will not be meager.

Life is rose leaves,
Losing all in old age,
Making dust that the earth receives,
Preparing the soul to produce its image.

Life is also a rose root,
Protected by mother earth,
Life is also a rose fruit,
To sweeten the world with mirth.

LINCOLN'S GIFT TO ME

As a slave, Lincoln set me free
From forced labor without a fee
And created my own name
One the master could not claim

To be master of my home
Wherever I choose to roam
Lincoln set me free, so I could learn
The true meaning of what education could earn

But to me Lincoln's greatest gift
Was to keep a family together and not drift
Far away, to be sold and to lose identity
But to create love bonds and fraternity

He taught me to be master of my fate
And praying to God at an early date
He taught me to respect my mate
Love my children at any rate.

Love my neighbors as myself
To build strong foundations for myself
And to share with all and loving all
He said with his lesson, I would never have to crawl.

Live Today

We only pass once this way
In this fleeting time scheme
We build hope and a dream
Of the very best for today
For there is no promise for tomorrow
Whether for happiness or sorrow
We alone are in a tidal wave
What will become of what we have?
For the future we will pray
What will be, will surely be
But God is standing by to see
He is the greatest equalizer of all
He lifts and breaks a fall
And says, just be thankful for today.

LIVE YOUR LIFE

Live your life as if today were the last
Greeting the sun and rain with equal power
Live your life today, not in the past
And with fresh inspiration like the April shower.

Live your life, with joy in your heart
Forgetting lost dreams of yesteryears
Live your life in God's living art
Of love, beauty and truth, without fears.

Live your life as a friend standing by the road
Greeting the travelers and cheering the weary
Live your life with all the goodness you can afford
The more you give, the more you smile,
your life won't be dreary.

Live your life, time is fleeting
The clocks are ticking, times will not repeat
Live your life, death is the last meeting
If we have loved well, we all will meet.

LOVE AND POWER

What makes one day different from another
The sun may shine, the rain may fall
The wind may whistle and travel farther
The water in the river may lead to a waterfall

What is the interpretation of life
Isn't it a combination of sorrow and felicity
Isn't life mixed with pleasure and strife?
Isn't it complicated, inconsistent and full of simplicity?

Is there a true definition of reality?
Yet Plato tries to make it clear
If we think of freedom and liberty
Can we count on luck to make it clear?

If we use our precious time to develop love
As Martin Luther King taught: love over power
King's gift of love is from above
Nietzsche's power is like a dead flower.

LOVE ME

Darling, love today, every day!
Put your arms around me and kiss,
Caress me, and treat me in thine own loving way,
Carry me over the bridge, over the rut, I am all with thee

To me some serenades sing!
To me your promises never break,
Into my life happiness bring,
And you I will never forsake

I mean love—love me!
Love me with all thy might!
Love me, oh I pray to thee,
Through the day, and through the night

Love me to honor and to adore,
Love me all through life,
Love me when we both stand at heaven's door
As we tell the master of all our strife!

Mamma Is In The Kitchen

Mamma is in the kitchen
Baking pies,
Mamma is in the kitchen
Chasing flies!
Her old gingham dress so neat and clean
She works with precision, yet unseen.

Mamma is in the kitchen
Cooking dinner,
Mamma is in the kitchen
So we won't be thinner,
Cleaning each plate and pan,
Making each child a woman or a man.

Mamma is in the kitchen
Singing a song,
Mamma is in the kitchen
All along,
She talks to God in an humble prayer
She does her duty with a stare.

Mamma is in the kitchen
Her work is almost done,
Mamma is in the kitchen
A race she has run
She never shirks from dawn to dawn
Her face is pleasant without a frown.

MASTER OF ALL

God sits in heaven, looking at us all
He holds us all steady before we fall
He plants knowledge in our minds
And grows love of many kinds

God uses his mighty spirit
To gain the love that we merit
To aid the traveler on his way
So he'll be thankful for a God-given day

God gives us the ability to heal
With His own 'loving spirit
He holds the sword and the shield
He gives us all that we merit.

MEDITATION

Let me grow old, but with grace
Let my eyes discern the sun, even if I am blind
Let my skin be wrinkled, but never without a smile on my face
These gifts I ask for in my good mind.

Let every word spoken or buried deep within
Be of help to lift some sunken spirit
Let every good soul unite and be kin
Or kind, for this is God's merit.

Let my life be an example of the best —
In friendship, in love, in hope and kindness
Let me give of myself so I can pass God's test
Let me be steadfast in God's fineness.

Oh God, as I think and pray
And examine the world with all its grief
Oh God, as I pray today
Taker care of me as you would a delicate leaf.

MELANCHOLY

Ah—you are so melancholy!
Are you alone? Are you afraid?
Are you burdened with some unholy care
That will soon fade?

Why do you sigh and weep?
Why do tears drop from your eyes?
The tear should vanish and a smile keep
And brighten up those eyes!

Sad you—somewhere the sun shines,
The stars are brighter at night,
Sad you—God holds the lines
And can banish sorrow out of sight!

Cheer up and be gay!
Make each day a little brighter,
God will lead you all the way!
He will make each day lighter and lighter.

Mother

Her hands so soft and warm
Her diamond sparkling eyes
The feel of her loving charm
Her love that overshadows my cries.

Her loving face of smiles and kindness
The kiss from her lips so tender
The love she gives without blindness
Her heart is pure, she is no pretender.

Her loyalty to good is steadfast
Her dreams are for her brood
To reach for the stars at last
And to uplift the world's neighborhood.

Her Brood, the treasure of her life
Is all she has to the world to give
They are her reflection of good and strife
They are her reason to survive.

MY CREED

Don't look to see my tears,
They are buried in my heart,
Don't look to see my fears,
They are not my art.

My love washes all evil away,
My kindness in full view,
My loyalty carries me through the day,
With courage there to renew.

The struggles I face throughout life,
Are paid with God's love that is full-fledged,
No one can turn away strife,
Nor can anyone tip my soul over the edge
I live in God's peace and beauty.

My Glory

My glory is not in a place so fine,
Nor in a lavish place where one can dine,
My glory is not in fancy talk,
Nor in high places where one can walk.

My glory is not in emulating another man,
Although his success is in demand,
My glory is not in dreams,
Nor spending time working out schemes.

My glory is not in wealth or gold,
At the risk of losing my soul,
My glory is not in gaining praise,
Or even in causing eyebrows to raise.

My glory is in my heart,
And all the world can be a part.

MY HEART

My heart is full of sunshine,
And all the stars so bright,
The four chambers are placed right.
One houses kindness,
One houses unselfishness,
And the partition line,
On the right side for hope,
On the left there is courage, which helps me cope,
There are layers and layers of love,
And justice in every curve,
The outer coating is loyalty so fine,
It glitters and startles the eye,
And here peace will forever lie,
There is no room for the unkind.

MY WANTS

I want someone who is kind,
Who appreciates the simple things in life
Someone who wouldn't mind
Giving a hand in times of strife.

Someone who is fancy or plain
But gives his fellow man his best
Someone who never complains
That he is better or worse than the rest.

Someone who is gentle and polite
Someone who accepts the sun and the rain the same
Someone who kisses me with delight
And blushes when he hears my name.

Someone to be near me and protect me
I mean an all-around friend
Someone who is beyond suspicion, you see
With this friend, God only makes the end.

MY WAY

When my needs are barely filled,
Or not filled at all:
My heart is never chilled.
As I do for others,
In answer to the Master's call.

When my pains seem too hard to bear
And obstacles keep coming my way,
I think of the love I can share
And all the pleasant words I can say.

When the blistering heat of the day,
The rain, the storms and winters cold,
I only think back to a spring day
When flowers grow and bloom so bold.

When all the good and bad are weighed
Justice seems to tip the scale
With all the joy and peace I have made
I have no time to sit and wail.

Neighbor

A neighbor is one who shares and loves
And respects his neighbor next door
And one as humble as a dove
No human being is a bore

A neighbor trusts another and is kind
In heart and in spirit above all
A neighbor is a servant, and king of mankind
A neighbor would climb a mountain to hear a call

He really knows his neighbor next door
He is there to comfort the sick, to share pain
He is there when needed as mentioned before
He is his brother's keeper, not seeking gain

A neighbor will hear a child's cry
A neighbor is there to comfort a widow
A neighbor soothes your heart and wipes your tears dry
And a neighbor is there when you are feeling low.

OF WHAT

We dread to look at new faces
We dread the daylight
We dread unknown distant places
We dread weakness and we dread might
We want a body free of pain
We welcome the sun and therein
We fear, oh God, the unknown
About heaven, there is so much talk
We are told to live right and watch our walk
We are told about heaven, but no one wants to die
We are even told that men never cry.

Ordinary People

Ordinary people are born equal and humble at birth
Born of parents filled with determination and worth
Who have made every day's work count
So his newborn's future would amount
To a higher plateau than his own
And make life for his brood un-torn
In this land filled with competition and greed
Where only successful planning will do the deed.

Ordinary people are born in a God-fearing home,
Where the ungodly would dare to roam,
Prayers of thanks at noontime
In the morning and evening for the relief of a crime.
Church on Sundays and work on Mondays
Giving their best, praying for love and for kindness always,
And doing the best for strangers and neighbors
And expecting a reward for these labors.

Ordinary people who when called to arms
Accept the call as part of their charms
Will stand up for their country anywhere
They know their duty and are always there
They will never let "Old Glory" be trampled on
They will fight till the battle is won
They work hard and strive for meritocracy
To remain strong and safe in this democracy.

They are ordinary people, you see,
They give birth to poets and presidents-to-be
They give birth to the doctor with healing hands
The artist who paints remembrances of the lands
They give birth to men who give spirit to the soul
And to the men who move silver and gold
The ordinary people are filled with wisdom
They are the meek and the stewards of the kingdom.

So let us all be up and going and be content
to be ordinary people
Let us walk in the footsteps of heavenly people
Let us feel good when the day is done
Knowing that we have done some good for someone
Let our dreams be for peace on earth and love
For all mankind, that his blessings flow from above
To all the ordinary people on earth who love
For they are the true stewards from birth.

Out Of Africa

Out of Africa, here we are
Chained into slavery, there was no law
No mercy shown, worked, beaten and scolded
Life's devastation and hardships unfolded

No stable family unit to protect us
No language worth saving, except that of the select
No new god but instead an earthly master
A whip, a plow, and Master says, "Work faster."

They can bear children, not really for them to keep
But to be put on the block and sold like sheep
No wife or husband to form a union of one
No permanent home to dwell in when the day was done

For spiritual songs, words were easy to find
And at night stories would come to mind
The tall tales and dances till sundown
But ears always listen for Master's sound

With Master's children in the classroom
There is the still, quiet sweep of the broom
The spelling of words to keep in the head
And a keen memory of every word read

The hiding of books and notes on paper
The concealing of learning was a terrible caper
To act dumb, and yet not be dumb
And always keeping the right action at your thumb

To learn to read and create a world of thought
The thought that multiplies more than what is taught
The question, oh the question of equality
The question, the question of justice and liberty

The burning desire deep in the dungeons of the heart
To share what I have learned from the start
To create long-lost family ties and paternity
And leave the best for my posterity.

PERFECT

Don't look for a perfect human being,
Because then, there would be nothing left to learn or to
teach,
Don't look for a perfect building,
There would be no improvements to make.

Don't look to the sun to shine always,
There is need for rain too,
Don't look for all the bright stars,
The darkness has its good too.

Don't look for life to be all smooth,
And for all the paths to be full of roses,
There would be no hearts to soothe,
Which life's fate never discloses.

Don't ever think that all things are the same,
And that things and time go through the same changes,
Just as the beginner artist obtains his fame,
Fall, Winter, Spring, and Summer rearrange.

PRECIOUS LORD

Precious Lord, there is beauty in Your home,
Precious Lord, who accepts all the blame,
We give thanks for your salvation,
We are grateful to be endowed with the greatest peace,
Through prayer there is great release,
Precious Lord, there is beauty in Your name,
Precious Lord, there is peace in Your fame.

Come on, come all, reveal,
Give heed to His call and kneel,
The King's heart is for the rich and poor,
There is no pay: He opens the door,
Precious Lord, there is beauty in His name,
Precious Lord, there is peace in His fame.

Come with a loving heart,
Come and do your part,
Come with malice toward none,
Come, a battle you have won,
Precious Lord, there is beauty in His name,
Precious Lord, there is peace in His fame.

When forever I close my eyes,
When I shall awake upon the skies,
God guide me to Your heavenly home,
When I will be with the saints to roam,
Precious Lord, there is beauty in His name,
Precious Lord, there is peace in His fame.

PRISONER

Man is a prisoner in his own home,
The doors are equipped with dead-bolt locks,
The windows are draped in iron bars,
And have sophisticated burglar alarms.

He is afraid to walk the streets,
As the dark nights set in,
He watches every stranger that he meets,
In the broad daylight hours.

He fears for his own life,
And that of his only family and possessions,
He tires of the strife,
Of continuously guarding his wealth.

He possesses good and decent morals,
He and his family worship in church,
Singing the songs of religious laurels,
He does his best and gives his best.

He wonders if the Decalogue is erased
From the memory of most people,
He remembers the robbers that he faced
And it was just by luck that he survived.

He remembers how it used to be,
When newspapers and milk were delivered to his door,
They are gone forever, never to be,
The victim of a street robber.

Only change in a man's heart,
The heart of the one who commits the crime,
Only the prayers of a religious heart,
Can change the temperament of the day.

Everyone can be a role model,
Everyone can walk in the footsteps of Christ,
Using the decalogue as a model,
To cleanse the heart of greed.

Reverend Preacher

Reverend, just a word about your sermon this morning!
You said up in heaven everybody is equal,
There is no need for burning, looting, and
no backdoor entrance —
But Reverend, I can't believe it —
Will the white folks be there too?

Reverend, you said there will be no separation
Everybody will live side by side,
But, Reverend, I can't believe that —
Not the way these white folks run from us down here,
You mean white folks will be in heaven too?

Reverend, you said there would be peace
And there would be eternal happiness
You mean to tell me there will be no wars
With the presence of the white man up there, too?

Reverend, your sermon was such a fantasy,
Seems to be right out of a childhood's wonderland —
How can you be sure of how it will be
In a place that you have not seen or been?
How do you know if these same white folks
will be in heaven too!

ROSES

I have seen roses in the spring
And birds flying over to sing
I have seen roses in the rain
And winds blowing in the lane

I have seen a bud peeping
Covered in green as if it was sleeping
I have seen a beautiful yellow rose
Lie quietly in repose

I have seen a white rose in all its beauty
Glistening with dew, I was satisfied of its purity
To lengthen the beauty of life
And throw off unneeded strife
But take a friendly advice
Its beauty will always suffice.

School Days Of Yesteryear

Books were a pleasure and not a privilege,
To be read in leisure and cared for by every child in the village,
Books were bought, they were not free,
So every parent sought for their due.

Teachers were a prize to be honored and adored,
No child by her side would ever be bored,
Because parents at home had much respect,
They taught their children, their lesson never to neglect.

There were no excuses for a bad grade,
Momma believed the words that the teacher made,
The people who believed the most in my life,
Were the teachers and the preacher of any style.

I would not exchange my old schooldays for those of today,
Nor would I exchange my old values for those of today,
The good old rules of long ago
Were respect for school and human dignity also.

SLEEP MARY SLEEP

Sleep, Mary, sleep, no more weeping
Your baby has been born, the shepherd are keeping
A watch over the manger today
And the stars are doing something magical today.

Sleep, Mary, sleep, and let there be peace on earth
Let all men glorify your child's birth
The Magi are on their way
Hosanna to your son today.

Sleep, Mary, sleep,
This child, so beautiful and mild
Has fulfilled the words of old
He is here, so bold.

Sleep, Mary, sleep, your son is here to stay
He is the ruler of the world forever today
Peace on earth, he gives the rod
For he is truly the Son of God.

SOLITUDE

In the quietness of the night
When the lights are dim and low
One thinks with all his might
Of things to forget, and things to adore

One thinks of the past in years
What time means when growing old
One thinks of the heartaches and the fears
But more of the love that has maintained the soul

One thinks of the morning as the beginning of life
The noon as full maturity
And evening as the end of joy and strife
Or of the acts of the heart's purity

One's mind wonders over the years
How was time spent—in doing good?
Was Jesus Christ involved in affairs
And were the just deeds understood?

STEREOTYPE

I saw a boy, ten years old, snatch a lady's purse,
Took her rings, those he sold on the corner
And he looked at me and started to curse
I saw his father staggering drunk, the mother crying, in tears
The house was littered with filth and smelt like junk
The surroundings asunder and without care
I saw grass growing on the ground
No flowers and no trees anywhere
Not even birds flying around
I saw the boy's mother murmur a word
A word wishful but plainly heard,
"O Lord," as she sadly dropped her head
I saw Cadillac cars brand new and shiny
I saw bars on the corners and pimps too
I saw the "pick-up man"
Collecting his numbers and bets for horse races,
I saw the dope addict recollecting
The familiar places
That he could rob to get money for a fix
I saw a politician in all this dismal misery
I saw a mortician, waiting for the corpse of this misery!

THANK YOU

Thank you for the candle
That makes a ray of light
Thank you for those who handle
And light their candles at night

Thank your for the birds that sing
Thank you for the drops of rain
The water from the spring
And the wildflowers in the lane

Thank you for the grain of sand
The morning dew, the rising sun
The setting sun all over the land
And thank you for a day well done

Thank you for the wild flowers
The trees, valleys and mountains
Thank you for the April showers
The rocks and the flowing fountains.

THE BIRDS

Sing, little birds, sing!
Let your voices echo among the trees:
Sing, little birds of spring
And arouse the honeybees!

Sing to me, little birds
Sing to the whole wide world:
Sing, let your melody be heard
And let every note be unfurled.

May every chirp be in harmony
And be thrilling to the ears!
May all chaos and agony
Be driven away through the years!

Little birds, forever sing,
Now and forevermore
Melodies forever bring,
You little birds are something to adore!

THE BLACK LEECH

The black leech has fathered children
But has little else
He has fluttered his time in foolish ventures
Thinking only of himself

Cadillacs and women are his thing
He never thinks of his brood
Poor mom is left on the mercy of welfare
The children run wild in the neighborhood

Sometimes children, despite obstacles,
Climb their way up to the top
They have earned their way no matter how hard
And feel quite humble even at the top

When they have made it to the top
The black leech tries to step in
He tries to lie to them about momma
It was she whom he blames for everything that happened.

He tries to bribe them with gifts
He offers the Cadillac and hides the women
He is always bragging, "These are my children."
This is very typical of the Black Leech-man.

THE DAY ON THE CROSS

I saw him carrying a heavy cross
I heard him groan and stumble, they pushed him away
But I saw the stones they cast
I even saw the crown of thorns that day.

I saw them when they nailed him to the cross
Between two ungodly thieves
I saw him faced by those so lost
And said, "Of this man, no one believes."

I saw him as they speared him on his side
I saw him in pain and agony
His face he never tried to hide
I saw them give him no sympathy.

I heard in a real soft voice, "Take my mother home."
This he told John, his disciple of choice
As he hung his head and with a moan, he said,
"It is finished! It is finished."

THE END

When we can hear a bird singing,
And maybe not anymore,
When we can hear the joy bell ringing,
Or maybe they are on a distant shore,
Stop! It is not the end.

When it seems that life is a pause,
And everything is at a standstill,
You can't think of the reason or cause,
And you stumble and falter at will,
Stop! It is not the end.

When it seems like it is the winter of life,
And spring forgot to shower her face,
When it seems like all efforts end in strife,
And happiness and joy have lost their place,
Stop! It is not the end.

Stop! Open up your windows,
Breathe fresh air and let the sun come in,
Hope and love always foreshadows
A good life to the end,
Stop! It is not the end.

THE ENGAGEMENT

The couple walked side by side,
They knew they wanted to abide
By love's great hand forevermore
As soon as one would open the door
To that great thought buried deep in each mind
A conscience that was not blind
To the conversation that had to begin
And gave no thought to when it would end

There were a few kisses, but more blushes,
The sweat, oh, how the body flushes!
The dedication to love dearly and to obey,
Through sickness, death, and all the way
And hold hands all through life
He, a husband, and she, a wife
Hear the sound of the wedding bells ring
And bring into the world new offspring.

Such relentless emotions and the display of devotion,
But who would take on the word portions?
Was this young girl prepared to say
The very words that seemed to go astray?
Will his glowing heart fill
When she gives the answer, "I will."
"Is this the night?" wonders she.
"Will he ask, 'Will you marry me?'"

The Garden Song

There is so much inspiration
In a garden, a garden!
There is so much concentration
In a garden, a garden!

A garden filled with roses,
Robins and their young reposes
In the garden, the garden!

There is so much pleasure
In the garden, the garden!
There is so much leisure
In the garden, the garden!

A garden filled with flowers,
Greeting the April showers —
The garden, the garden!

THE HUMMINGBIRD

Oh, the hummingbird so wise
Oh, the hummingbird so pretty and so small
Knows the sweetest flower of all
Oh, the hummingbird is always in motion
His long bill gets a potion
Of the sweetest nectar which is the prize
His motions are tireless
And his piercing eyes are tireless
His sounds are recognized
His small body can be visualized
Whoever believes that little bird
With motions that speak for words
Can create a world of wonder?
For he is real, God does not blunder.

The Impression

You looked at my skin with deep pigmentation
A head full of kinky hair
A nose that is flat and large
A mouth with thick lips
And teeth as white as ivory
I was different and you turned away.

You looked at my buttocks
So round and thick
You looked at a body robust and brawny
And at feet that seemed to carry a ton
I was different and you turned away.

You couldn't see the love in my eyes
Because you had one in your heart
You couldn't see the kindness in my heart
Because your heart was made of stone
I was different and you turned away.

The skill of my mind, you cared not to penetrate
Rather than being healed by my hands,
you preferred to be sick
Before you could shake my hands, you took another direction
Rather than sit by me, you preferred to stand
I was different and you turned away.

THE LUMP

One day I felt a lump
Somewhere in my throat
The lump was not of a physical nature
The exact feeling, I cannot say

The feeling of hurt was in knowing
That my heart that is too often filled with joy
Had wished for a coldness to begin growing
This act of un-thoughtfulness has taken all my joy

I wished it had been a physical lump
For I can seek medical care
But actions or unkind words cannot be recalled
They remain and hurt like a spear.

THE MAN OF WEALTH
WITHOUT MERCY

The man of wealth lives in his home,
With his family and has servants galore,
But now free is he to roam,
And not worry about his wealth in store.

How can he feel free enough
To take his foot off an underling's neck?
How can he face the rough
And allow every man a decent check?

How can he have his cupboards full
Of good food and the finest drinks?
How can he smile when his pockets are full
With unclean money and gold cuff links?

How can he sleep well at night
Knowing that he has turned a shoddy deal?
Or maybe he has taken the last widow's smile,
And in prayer never kneels.

Does wealth make a heartless man
Or turn him into stone?
Does wealth make a ruthless man
And make him feel he holds all the power above?

THE MARIGOLD

Ah, you little marigold,
You even smile in the rain!
Your face of beautiful shining gold,
You even grow in the lane!

You seem to laugh at sorrow,
You laugh with the sun,
You bloom through tomorrow
And many a heart you have won!

Dear Marigold—forever bloom
Give joy to the depressed,
May your beauty loom
And may your seeds germinate the best!

May your smiles stay
In your blossoms forevermore,
You are autumn's queen so gay
You are the prize of the show!

The Millionaire

From the earth
He finds wealth,
The scheming, dreaming millionaire.

He mines the coal and the ore,
Sulphur, salt, and much more
The scheming, dreaming millionaire.

He builds the bridges and the rails,
He builds the tunnels and makes sails
The scheming, dreaming millionaire.

He does his part
With the earth's art,
The scheming, dreaming millionaire.

The earth is free for all
And her fortunes are there at anybody's call
The scheming, dreaming millionaire.

It beckons you to scan
Every inch that you can
To be a scheming, dreaming millionaire.

The Path of Life

Only the wise find out,
That life's path isn't smooth at all,
Sometimes one stumbles and sometimes one falls,
Sometimes one smiles and sometimes shouts,
Sometimes one shakes his head and pouts,
Sometimes I feel like the sun has lost its splendor,
And rain and gloom becomes life's order,
One asks himself, "Is this what life is about?"
But one should never lower his head,
But greet the rain and sun just like a board,
Learning from the past and looking to the future,
Love and goodness one should wed,
Hope and courage should be sung aloud,
For the path of life is good and strong and true.

JONETTA W. SINGLETON

THE POLITICIAN

Vote for me, I am one of your brothers
I will get legislation for civil rights,
Plenty of jobs and housing that's equal to others
And a voice that has never articulated your plight
Just vote for me and you will see.

Vote for me, I will use the filibuster
On laws that are not to your benefit
I will articulate our sensitivity to those power leaders
And I will guarantee to you that I won't be a misfit
Just vote for me.

Vote for me, just look at my credentials
I was in the civil rights struggle, I am a lawyer
Look at my family—that is essential
Vote for me, I will not leave you waiting in the foyer,
Your answer will come, if you will only vote for me.

Well, we voted for you, you won big
We voted for you, you are our man
Your promises, we are waiting to dig
Jobs are our priority and demand
So we voted and put you in.

Public works bill, you voted the other way
Housing, you say this isn't the time
Equal rights, you forgot that day
You lack persuasion, this is a crime
You use too much of your time chatting with Whitey.

We send you telegrams and letters
We also make telephone calls to you
There is no response; we could have used our vote better
We were fooled when we voted for you.

We wanted you because you were one of us
You missed your appointment, we had to talk to you
You preferred playing golf and evaded us
Have you turned white too
Just because we voted for you?

We can't call for your impeachment
Because your sins are only of omission
Rather than blatant commitment
You failed to carry out your mission
We were misled when we voted for you.

The Saintly Soul
And The Stranger

Here is a story about a saintly soul
Who lived by the side of the road
To greet the passersby, I am told
He did his cooking early in the morn
As he hummed a familiar song
He cleaned his house and he swept his yard
He watered his favorite goldenrod
And spread his yard with fresh sod.

He would sit at his bay window
As he had done years before
And watch for a stranger on the road
To show his face and rest his load
On this the summer's hottest day
When flowers are withering and grass turns to hay
And the mockingbird looks for a shady place
And all the noontime bells give a muffled ring.

In his favorite chair at the window he would stare
To ask this unknown stranger to share
His cool home, and at his table, share a meal
A change of raiment, a prayer, to kneel
This was the life of the saintly soul
And much more, still untold
For his greater soul lies within
And all his goodness is filled therein.

He did see a traveler with a sagging back
You could tell he was no reveler from the looks of his pack
As he slowly approached him and called
He turned to him, and he saw his soiled shawl
He looked into his eyes, but the stranger's eyes
looked like piercing arrows
He looked up at the skies and tried to gather some
thoughts to appease his sorrows
But there were none; this was a strange man indeed
He wondered to himself, whether he or the
stranger were in need.

He grabbed for the stranger's hand for him to shake
Oh, how the magnetic heat from the stranger's
hand seemed to bake
His hand, such a strange feeling
When he began to stumble, and his head went reeling.

The Sparrow and the Dove

One day I saw a sparrow
Fall from the sky with a bang!
I rushed over to hear his sorrow
And to inquire about the rest of the gang.

The sparrow had been doing well,
But had followed his friends a little out of the way
And got into mischief too bad to tell
That is why he was down that day

Sympathizing with him, here comes a hawk
And then another one so big and strong
There on earth they started to squawk
They said the sparrow had done them wrong.

I tried my best to get away
But the hawks were too strong
On the sparrow's shoulders I tried to lay
But he had not the strength to defend his own wrong.

I was beaten by the hawks, but a lesson I have learned
Be not so quick to lower yourself for someone
To remove these scars I have yearned —
To help a weakling is no fun.

The Things I Want To Do
Satisfactorily

Let me sniff the freshest flower
And enjoy the morning sun
Let me welcome a fine April shower
Let me have peace when the day is done.

Let there always be an abundance of love
Let my friendship be loyal and true
Let the good Master above
Guide my life so sure and true.

Let me think alone, all alone
Of the long highway of life
Let me forget hatred no matter where I roam
And see beauty amid strife.

Let me give out the best love
No matter what I get in return
Let me be thankful to the Master above
And not for one moment from him turn.

THE TWO PHILOSOPHERS

Mr. Bee and Mr. Fly

Mr. Bee

I work so hard all day,
Gathering pollen from all the flowers,
Building hives, I know the way;
I help to enforce her powers.

I help to make the finest wax;
My honey from pollen is so sweet.
But you, Mr. Fly, what makes you act
And look like nothing, you are incomplete.

Mr. Fly

Mr. Bee, you are judging me by my looks;
You don't know anything about me.
But please go and get your books;
In them I am a hero, you will see.

Did not the great Italian man
Through long days of observation
With a great study in his hands
Prove to be my ovation?

THE VIETNAM DEAD SOLDIER
(IN ARLINGTON CEMETERY)

We are the flowers
Kissed by the midnight dew
And cuddled by the morning sun
We are the flowers bathed
By an April shower
And greeted by the soft voices of the wind
We are honored to be in this garden
For God knows what
To keep watch over forevermore.

We don't know why we are here
But we must keep our spirit high
We throw off good pollen to attract bees and butterflies
We must invite the nightingales
And the robins to sing
A dolorous song forevermore
A dolorous song forevermore.

We once lived, had dreams
And had visions,
We were young and full of laughter
We were bright and in our youth
We had so much to give and receive
But now we are flowers
To keep watch over this garden
Forevermore! Forevermore!

The Voice

A voice tells you what to write —
You have a perceptive insight
But your temperament is lazy
Which makes everything hazy.

You don't know, careless you,
What you are bringing into the world —
Great thoughts — are an asset to all
With them, you rise or fall.

Ah, great writers are fighters, too
They fight their battles through
Only God sends them hope and inspiration
To carry out his administration

The task is great, the reward small
But that's his fate; he answers the call
He writes for God out of his soul
He is eccentric, and yet so bold.

THE WEEPING WILLOW

Cheer up, weeping willow
You are beautiful even with tears—
Your twigs are greenish yellow
You bring hope that inhibits man's fears.

Your trunk looks at the sky
Your leaves point to the earth
You bow as if to pray or cry
But you are giving hope a new birth.

Weeping willow, forever stand
You are in complete simplicity
You are nursed by God's own hand
You are with complete felicity.

One hundred years or more
Be an umbrella for the young and old
May your radiance forever glow
And you can stand forevermore.

Theories

Theories come and theories go;
They are tested one by one every day;
Life is full of friends and foes;
For they are constant all the way.

The sun will shine if not today;
Day follows night and time passes away;
The Winter will come and Spring will follow;
Summer and Fall is for the parade of swallows.

Life is temporary, but death is eternal;
Birth and death are cheerful absolutes;
The earth to both provides material;
We dream of each other's results.

The wind blows to and from yonder shores;
It brings rain to make flowers grow;
The stars that shoot across the sky glows;
This is God's work, and what is more?

THREE POTS OF GOLD

I found three pots of gold;
I found them at the end of a rainbow —
I will tell this story to you, dear soul
And all my gold, I have to show.

The first pot, believe me,
Was large, radiant, and bright
Full of love so plain to see,
It even shines at night.

As I look a little farther, real hard,
I spied a pot called loyalty, so great
This very pot, I yelled aloud!
It was for my fellow man, small or great.

Then there was another pot called kindness;
Its gold was as bright as the sun —
Hatred was forgotten in the blindness
As my day was completely done.

These three pots of gold, my friend,
I shall treasure all my life;
These three pots of gold, my friend,
Can carry me through any strife.

TIME

When on a given day,
Life takes on a saddened feeling
Of lost memory, and joy takes a long delay,
Which leaves the soul shocked and reeling.

When at a given hour,
Hope seems so far and fading;
Gaining happiness is not in your power;
Life's bitter changes you are dating.

When at a given minute,
You have nothing to gain from the past;
You haven't thought hard, you do admit
That the good leaps from memories past.

When the last second has come,
The wish remains for hope, not pain;
When God with His mighty wisdom
Gives courage to rain as well as to the sun.

To Our Father

Dear Little Lover, the greatest
Just straight from heaven's door
Only God made you my mate
For us to be together forevermore.

So humble, thoughtful and polite
Brave, honest and fair;
You do the little things with much delight,
And give more than your share.

You who labor through toil and strife,
Do your best and never shirk at all;
Look to God for eternal life
And to guide your feet that you may not fall.

Yes, you, my children's day is awake—
We want you to know that you are our stake
You are alive—so smell our flowers.

Unthoughtful Actions
and Words

Unthoughtful words and actions
Shatter hopes and hurt feelings,
Cause pains and aggravations
And make the heart question the dealings.

Unthoughtful words and actions may be unplanned
But carelessly perpetrated, not
Intended to hurt a single soul in the land
But the victim is chagrined in a knot.

Unthoughtful words and actions leave an imprint
And always strike a downward note
They cannot be called back even if you repent
For on the heart, it is wrote

So let us all forever strive
To eliminate unthoughtful words and actions
And let there not be bad thoughts to revive
For I have rendered kind words and thoughtful actions.

Virtue

What do I get in return?

Divided my raiment with the poor,
Helped the beggar who came to my door.
My rewards I did not earn;
I gave what I had with a smile;
To help the sick I walked a mile;
I washed wounded and sick men's feet;
I cleaned the bed, I gave them bread;
The welfare of others is my concern;
Yet I see all around me,
The rich get richer—it's there to see;
I want no thanks and never yearned for a reward;
I want no one to push me forward;
Just let me do God's will at every turn.

Visiting a Strange Land

When I travel to a strange land
And I know not one man
I think of the things I left behind
And look for similar things to find

I think first of nature's gift
Of the sun, the moon and the stars, and my spirit lifts
I hear the sound and the patter of rain
I see the bird pecking on my window pane

I see the children's kites in the sky
I see the smoke from chimneys going so high
I see people coming and going in market places
In a conglomeration of races

I see bands marching to a familiar tune
And flowers blooming as in June
I see babies being born everyday
And funeral possessions along the way

I see there are also evil minds
I also see that goodness outshines
And will be the conqueror in the end
There will be no wrong to defend.

WE ARE A PEOPLE

We are a people with pigmented skin
Curly hair, big lips and teeth of ivory
We stand tall in good deeds, as other men
We will defend our country's glory.

We are a people of flesh and not stone
We are a people of will, a people of virtue
A people who stand tall but not on thorn
And a people full of truth and beauty and with a soul so true.

We are a people who have been mistreated
Denied justice and equality
We have been made a scapegoat whenever it fits the need
But we continue to pray to God for liberty.

We have waited through long days and nights
For a chance to take our first steps in a thousand miles
For the distance that will ensure our rights
In this land that's filled with hatred and a few smiles.

We are the people whose flesh has been pricked
By the pins of hatred, and it still bleeds
We are the people who have felt the kicks
From the doors of opportunity, and no one
pushed for our needs.

We are the people who grow old and weary
Sickened with broken promises and hope
We are the people skeptical and leery
We are the people who pray to God for the will to cope.

WE ARE THANKFUL

For the little stubborn sun rays
That pierce through dark clouds
For the stars that glitter always
For the moon that controls tides without delays,
We are thankful.

For the little drops of rain
For the wind that blows from far away
For fields that house the grain
For the pebbles, sand and the clay,
We are thankful.

For the food and the drink
For the home and good friends
For the wisdom you gave us to think
And for those with the strength of your hands you mend,
We are thankful.

For the love you have instilled in our soul
For the truth and beauty all around
For the chance to be in your fold
And to know that it is you, the greatest giver ever found,
We are thankful.

WHEN WE GET UP THERE

Dear Lord,

Are there any turnip greens and sweet potatoes
To eat as we enter the pearly gates?
And what about the chitterlings and chicken?
These are the foods of which we black people partake.

Dear Lord,
Will we be able to exchange
Our golden slippers for blue suede shoes and patent
leather?
And the white robes for pants and dresses
And hats and coats that are all-weather?

Dear Lord,
Instead of golden harps and trumpets
Can we exchange them for the record players and
television?
And have Cadillacs instead of golden chariots?
Lord, please let us make these simple revisions.

Dear Lord,
Will the white folk start running
When we enter your pearly gates?
The ground is gold so the grass can't run
But I believe those white folks will leave through the back gate.

WILD FLOWERS

I love to pick wild flowers
On the land or in a green forest
I love the smell of the flowers after an April shower
It is just a gift of nature's best.

I love the flowers, they are self-sufficient
They need no special help
The work of soil, rain and sun is so efficient
God only knows how they are kept.

I love the wild flowers, for they are humble
They stand and only weep with the rain and dew
I love the wild flowers, they cannot mumble
If they lack of food, water and sun — as we do.

I love the wild flowers for their fate
Their flowers do not last long enough
But remember, spring is the date
When they will show their face even if spring is late.

I love the wild flowers so fair
Their beauty is so true
Their fading is like death so near
Death that we will face some day too.

I will love the wild flowers forevermore
From bloom to flower, it will haunt my memory
When I shall pass to the other shore
In my heart, they will be my glory.

Wisdom

Oh, hear the voice of her calls
The beautiful voice of the sage
The voice so old with age
The voice that has uplifted my fall
That God installed to teach
And has been put in every man's reach
No matter how tall, low or small.

The voice of wisdom is for all to grasp
Whether one is strong or weak
Wisdom is in all our talks
And keep us straight in our walk
Not for the world to see its pride
But to guide along a heavenly ride.

WITH THESE HANDS

When I was a little child
I came inside from playing in the wild
I saw old granny, she looked so tired
Her smiles were loved and so admired.

I saw granny give me a kiss
And it would be ridiculous if she would miss
The child with a wounded hand
Or one who could get a sturdy foot on land.

Granny makes any food taste good
We always thought it should
Plum puddings and orange marmalades
And pies and all kinds of cakes baked with wood.

But who is this granny so divine?
Has she tasted the wine and the rine?
Has she been up and down?
Has she made her start from the ground?

YOUR PROMISE TO ME

You promised to make every day
In my life a very happy one;
You promise to drive the night away
In some far distant place to run.

You promised to shower me with kisses,
Caress me and never leave me alone
Alone to dream of the things my life misses
And for their presence moan.

You promised to be near me, or be not too far away
So you could easily hear my call;
And between us, there would never be a war—
Together, we would stand or fall.

All these promises were broken! Broken!
With deceit and lies from you;
But I shall remember them as a token
Because they came from you.